GREETINGS FROM
CHICAGO

Bruce Marshall

THUNDER BAY
P·R·E·S·S

San Diego, California

The Emergence of a City

How Chicago took advantage of a key location

If ever there was a case of the right place at the right time, it was here, in Chicago—an insignificant military outpost built at the foot of the Great Lakes early in the nineteenth century. The vulnerable and unfortunate Fort Dearborn made way for a trading settlement—and the spectacular potential here arose from its position on a continental divide, giving waterway routes into both the Mississippi–Missouri river complex, and into the Great Lakes, at the moment when interstate trade was taking off.

In August 1833, with business burgeoning, a dozen or so residents gathered to incorporate the town of Chicago. Fast forward, and their children's children greeted the next century alongside two million other Chicagoans. By

Above: Randolph Street in the 1850s, a key thoroughfare dating from the founding of the city. It later became the heart of the theater district.

1900 Chicago was indisputably the Second City of the United States and, indeed, the fifth-most populous metropolis in the world. As visualized by its founders, it had become the hub of the continent's trading.

Fourteen percent of the world's railroad traffic passed through its noisy, grimy yards where a maze of tracks sorted themselves into unhindered routes leading west to San Francisco and Los Angeles, south to New Orleans and Miami, and east to New York, Boston, and Montreal. And nature—with a little, later help from canal-builders—brought international maritime traffic to its doorstep, by way of the Great Lakes.

The rich output of the great agricultural region of the northern Mississippi Valley passed this way. Here were the world's largest grain and livestock markets (the 500 acres of the Union Stock Yards could house 400,000

Right: Maxwell Street, now lost and lamented, was a haven for European refugees, particularly Jews whose Sunday market created a city tradition.

Left: The artists and lithographers of the printmakers Currier and Ives recorded the city's energetic recovery from the Great Fire. This print was made in about 1880.

Below: The heart of the town as proponents of the Chicago School of architecture make their mark.

animals at a time). Whole forests arrived by rail and boat and departed as sawn lumber. Local resources of ore and soft coal fed the biggest steel-rolling mills.

Right place, right time.

Early History

A boomtown arises from the ashes

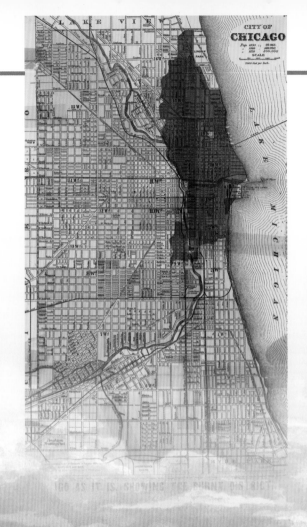

While this was the nineteenth-century's great Boomtown, it was not, naturally, a salubrious place to live. Underfoot, prairie bogs fostered breeding grounds for hostile insects, and low-lying land subject to spring flooding made dirt roads impassable. Immigration was on such a scale that services were overwhelmed: the sewage disposal problem became so desperate that waste pipes were laid across the city above ground. (Trenches were never dug for them; instead the city, in an early expression of the "can-do" spirit that would color its story, covered them by raising its street levels several feet.)

Thus the Great Fire of 1871, cruel and tragic though it was, can be seen as a watershed in the city's development, marking a new beginning. The blaze cleared four square miles—the whole of the central business district, stores and offices, workshops and warehouses, private mansions, and ghetto hovels—about a third of the city's property valuation.

Within days, Potter Palmer, the ashes of whose newly opened hotel were still smoldering, was rebuilding it across the street. Far-sighted and fastidious men who had made

Below: The Great Fire raged out of control until rain came to the rescue after two days. This was a city of wood. Stone and brick would be the rebuild materials.

Right: The red area shows the extent of the fire.

Above: Citizens flee the flames. There was panic among them when the fire jumped the Chicago River. About 100,000 were left homeless; 200–300 died.

fortunes in dirty, grimy, cut-throat businesses set about giving Chicago a jump-start toward being a fully rounded city community.

Within very few years of its 1892 founding, for instance, the University of Chicago had international status to match that of centuries-old British and European colleges. The city's public library housed 350,000 books in 1908.

The Art Institute of Chicago took it upon itself to teach the nation's teachers how to teach drawing in public schools.

The bold benefactors of these institutions wanted them dressed in suitably impressive fashion, and merchant adventurers aspired to commercial premises as grand as their ambitions, including department stores for Marshall Field and Carson Pirie, and storage for the inventory of the extraordinary new mail order merchants, Sears, Roebuck.

The young architects who gathered to serve them—Louis Sullivan from Philadelphia, the local boy Daniel Burnham, and John

Wellborn Root from New York—were soon producing the finest architecture in the nation, inaugurating the first Chicago School (there would be a second, led by Mies van der Rohe, Frank Lloyd Wright, and Buckminster Fuller, in the 1950s).

Left: The city marked its centennial with the World's Fair of 1933. Forty years earlier, Chicago had hosted the World's Columbian Exposition which introduced the Ferris Wheel as a fairground attraction.

Below: Michigan Avenue is known for up-market stores, historic and cultural centers, a famous bridge, and mansions and elegant spaces. Home to the Magnificent Mile, it's the Chicago street best-known to the world.

Reaching for the Sky

Architects find new ways of taking the strain

There were frustrating restrictions for the eager young architects who were rebuilding Chicago after the Great Fire. With land prices soaring, low buildings were an inefficient use of ground space. But ten stories was as high as they could go with traditional construction: load-bearing walls took the weight of everything above them. Furthermore, even those weights were on shaky ground hereabouts due to prairie bog, unstable soil and sand, and bedrock was 50 feet down. Caissons were required—monster pads of concrete settled into the swamp, spreading the weight of the buildings.

By now, Elisha Otis was marketing his failsafe elevators to find ways of going higher. The architects Burnham & Root decided to risk it, to go to 17 stories, the old-fashioned way.

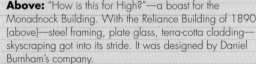

Right: The revered Water Tower brought Chicago its first clean drinking water, and survived the Great Fire. It is dwarfed now by the John Hancock Tower (background, left) and Water Tower Place.

Above: "How is this for High?"—a boast for the Monadnock Building. With the Reliance Building of 1890 (above)—steel framing, plate glass, terra-cotta cladding— skyscraping got into its stride. It was designed by Daniel Burnham's company.

Chicago Water Tower	Home Insurance Building	The Rookery	Auditorium Building	Masonic Temple	The Ferris Wheel	LaSalle-Monroe Building

250

200

150

100

50

m

Right: Skyline statements: the famous clock of the Wrigley Building, and "gothic" flying buttresses for the Chicago *Tribune*.

Below: William Wrigley demonstrated the profitability of chewing gum by installing golden front doors. Both buildings were constructed in the 1920s.

To support its own weight, the Monadnock Building's walls had to be six feet thick at the base. The finished construct, in fact, sank, requiring steps down to the doors.

    That was 1891. The same year, at the same location, 53 West Jackson Boulevard, work started on a southern half of the building. It would look much the same, but it was based on steel frame construction. The die was cast.

Wrigley Building

London Guarantee Building

Allerton Crowne Plaza

Metropolitan Tower

Chicago Temple Building

1540 North Lake Shore Drive

Roanoke Building

On the Up and Up

Achieving "the finest architecture in the nation"

William Le Baron Jenney was perhaps the true skyscraper pioneer. He had studied in Paris alongside Gustave Eiffel, builder of the world's most famous iron structure, and when in 1884 the Chicago-based Home Insurance Company commissioned an office block from him, Jenney planned for an iron frame. He was offered steel instead—more expensive but with the timely claim to be fireproof. A slim skeleton of it could hold the building up, allowing thin curtain walls—even just sheets of glass—to hang from the cross beams.

The "pyramid tradition"—the need for massive load-bearing bases for tall buildings—was over. This was "the most important innovation in the art of building since the Gothic cathedral," and the architecture of Chicago was primed to enter its golden age.

However, even Jenney balked at discarding all past tradition—he dressed the Home Insurance Building in reassuring brick and stone—and it was a while before the Chicago School would actually flaunt the design potential of metal, their new default material. The possibilities were sharp corners, sinuous curves, and even ornamentation by rivet-head.

Daniel Burnham and John Wellborn Root showed the way with the Reliance Building of 1895, whose protruding, angular bay windows highlight just how much glass the structure could bear. As for curves, Parisian architects had been the first to exploit the soft shaping that could be had from iron and steel: thus, Art Nouveau, which arrived in Chicago as stairway balustrades and elevator grills.

However, there wasn't much space for exterior ornamentation on these new towers: the expanses of glass were in themselves the

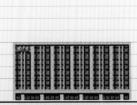

400						
350						
300						
250						
200						
150						
100						
50						
m	CNA Plaza	Unitrin Building	Marina Towers	CNN Realtors Building	The Newport North	The Newport South	2500 North Lake

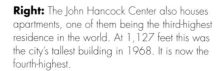

proud display. Air-conditioning had yet to arrive, so the Chicago Window became an iconic feature: a large central pane of glass flanked by narrower, opening sash windows.

But it was, of course, the pursuit of height that had the world watching. This was not merely bravado. It was the way to get more use out of every square foot of ever more expensive land, especially in the Loop, the increasingly crowded business district. First to rise above the spire of St. Michael's Church (290 feet) was the Board of Trade Building of 1885, reaching 322 feet. Though this was steel-framed, it was granite infilled. The Wrigley Building of 1922 was 100 feet higher than that. Creation of the world's tallest, densest skyline was under way.

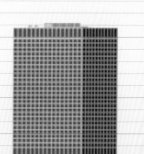

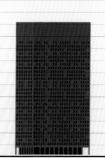

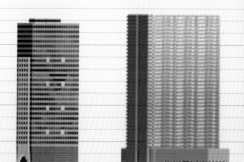

Chase Tower

John Hancock Center

200 West Jackson

One Illinois Center

150 North Wacker

Malibu East

Great Heights

How "less is more" became the talk of the town

Following the Great Depression and World War II, a new generation of Chicago architects emerged—to pioneer again, to lead the world again, to boast again. (Remember, one explanation of the nickname "the windy city" is that it derives from "windy citizens," a comment on the hubris of Chicagoans.)

The inspiration for the new movement, the Second Chicago School, came from Mies van der Rohe, a refugee from Nazi Germany who had arrived in Chicago as the head of the architectural school of the Armour Institute of Technology (later Illinois Institute of Technology, ILT). There, he rebuilt the campus, bravura work that was noticed by a property developer, Herbert Greenwald—hence the commission for a high-rise apartment block at 860–880 Lake Shore Drive, which was followed by, among others, the Chicago Federal Center and IBM Plaza.

The "Miesian" style was now truly on show, added to by his students and disciples. "Less is more" was the motto, but the "less," straight-sided rectangular blocks, displayed the richest materials: gleaming stainless steel and vast walls of tinted glass (as in his seminal Seagram Building in New York). The towers were placed, like sculptures, on stilts in landscaped plazas.

There was some critical reaction to the Miesian ethic: that it did not distinguish apartment block from office, from convention center, from college hall. "Symbolic neutrality" was the phrase. The Postmodernists came along to revise that.

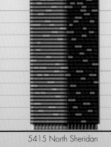

| 500 |
| 450 |
| 400 |
| 350 |
| 300 |
| 250 |
| 200 |
| 150 |
| 100 |
| 50 |
| m |

2400 North Lakeview · Elm Street Plaza · Regents Park North · Northern Trust Building · 5415 North Sheridan · Newberry Plaza · Willis Towera · 1555 North Astor

Above: The view from the top of the town. The observation deck of the Willis (formerly Sears) Tower is at 1,353 feet.

Above: The Trump Tower rises and rises—but not to the intended height; the design was scaled down after 9/11.

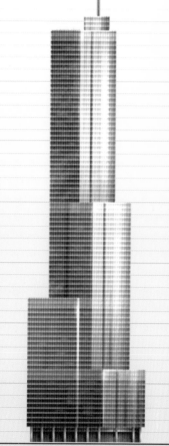

5 North Wacker   353 North Clark   Central Park One—Museum Park   300 North LaSalle   Aqua   Trump International Hotel & Tower

Blues

Imported music that Chicago made its own

Music accompanied the early twentieth-century African American migration from Mississippi Delta poverty to the promise of the industrial north. Its genre was Delta blues, a soulful sound made by guitar and harmonica.

In Chicago it picked up power with microphone and amplifier, adding drums, piano, and sometimes brass, but Chicago blues remained an ethnic interest, confined to the Black enclaves of the South Side where white people did not go. (Also settling in Chicago at the time was the hot jazz style of New Orleans Dixieland, which would make stars

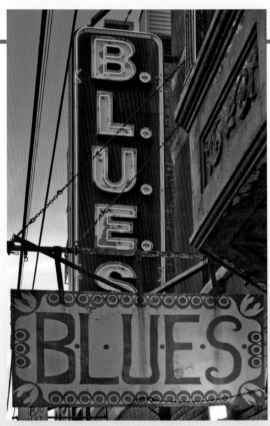

Above and left: Blues clubs kept the music alive, and revitalized it, as composer, guitarist, and lecturer Fernando Jones (left) does now. His book *I Was There When The Blues Was Red Hot* is an acknowledged authoritative work on the subject.

of King Oliver, Jelly Roll Morton, and Louis Armstrong.)

It was not until World War II that the sound of the blues could be heard across ethnic frontiers. Local phonograph labels like Bluebird, then Chess and Cobra, recorded Memphis Minnie, Muddy Waters, Jimmy Rogers, Bo Diddley, and found radio disc

As one grateful musician said, "a sweet home for the blues"

jockeys with airtime to fill. The growing Black community was spreading out; their style of blues clubs began to appear downtown and on the North Side, attracting audiences of not only non–African American locals but international visitors (who would then detect

Above: Jimmy Burns, seen here at Buddy Guy's Legends club, specializes in soul blues and electric blues.

this musical influence in the work of the Beatles and the Rolling Stones).

Chicago blues provided building blocks for soul and rock 'n' roll; BoogieWoogie emerged from the blues. Chicago blues joins the First Chicago School of architecture as the city's major contributions to modern American culture.

Left: Robert Lockwood Jr. has a jazz-influenced blues style. He was the first to play amplified blues on the radio, in 1942.

Right: The Auditorium Building of 1891 has National Historic Landmark status. Its theater was intended for "high culture" such as opera, but in the late 1960s it became Chicago's premier rock venue.

Curtain up on a lively scene of sounds and sights

The first complete symphony heard in Chicago—Beethoven's Second—was performed by the Germania Orchestra, a touring group of immigrant Germans, in 1853. Regular concerts by amateur musical societies and choruses teased the citizens' taste for music, but the true overture was heard in 1891 when the promise of artistic freedom and a well-paid, full-time orchestra tempted the conductor Theodore Thomas from New York. The Chicago Orchestra was born; it would become the Chicago Symphony Orchestra of international renown.

Ballet and opera made more labored progress, with financial difficulties overwhelming one effort after another. It was not until the 1950s that the Lyric Theatre of Chicago, later to

Above right: Picasso was owed $100,000 for his Civic Center sculpture. He donated the fee to the city's poor.

Above: A New York billboard for Chicago's own show, *Chicago*. Its murderous "heroines" are two young women of the Prohibition era.

Right: *Ferris Bueller's Day Off* featured Chicago landmarks including the Willis Tower, the Tribune Tower, the Stock Exchange, the Art Institute, and Wrigley Field.

Right: Rock band Chicago was formed by a group of six Chicago university students, originally called The Big Thing.

Left: Maria Callas made her U.S. debut in Chicago in the Lyric Opera's production of Bellini's *Norma*.

Below: Locations for the movie *The Blues Brothers* included the Richard J. Daley Center, City Hall, and Chicago's many back alleys.

be the Lyric Opera, took firm root in the city's cultural life. The Chicago Opera Ballet, in alliance with the Lyric, had a dance repertoire based on operatic plots and scores. A Chicago City Ballet company performed Balanchine's works immaculately, but tottered financially. Today, the Chicago Festival Ballet takes a repertoire around the country; the Joffrey Ballet, the "no star–all star" company based itself in Chicago in 1995.

More than 200 drama groups and companies, widely spread, underpin local theater, and their improvisational styles are said to be Chicago's unique contribution to the performing arts. Mainstream theater is concentrated in and around the Loop. Shakespeare's characters strut the stage at a permanent home on Navy Pier. The Jeff Awards are Chicago's equivalent of New York's Tonys.

Public art is one of the city's proudest features, with works by Chagall, Picasso, and Joan Miró to grab the attention of passers-by. And, once again, there is a heritage based on

the generosity of fastidious men made rich in the years of Chicago's explosive growth. Marshall Field's department store sponsored a fine-arts gallery until the 1950s. Other patrons returned from their European travels with masterpieces from every school from Old Master to Impressionist, and furnished the Art Institute of Chicago—itself founded by local artists—with enviable treasures.

Right: Daniel Barenboim served as music director of the Chicago Symphony Orchestra from 1991 to 2006.

Baseball

Loyalties on two sides of the city

Comiskey Park and Wrigley Field, homes of the two Chicago Major League Baseball franchises, make very different impressions on the urban scene.

Comiskey Park, the South Side venue for White Sox games (they were the White Stockings until newspaper headline writers shortened the name), was rebuilt in 1991 and its hi-tech modern 68-foot-wide scoreboard keeps spectators up to date via 900,000 LED lights. It also displays that most modern commercial phenomenon: a new identity to suit a naming sponsor—

Above: Ernie Banks, "Mr Cub," is honored at Wrigley Field. He was the Cubs' first black player and spent his entire major league career (1953–71) there.

Above: Frank Leroy Chance, the "Peerless Leader" of the Cubs in the 1900s. He played first base while managing the team to four National League championships.

U.S. Cellular Field—"the Cell" to fans. On the other hand, the Cubs' North Side home, Wrigley Field, still bears the name of the sportsman who bought it in the 1920s. And it prides itself on preserving links with that past. Set in a residential neighborhood rather than a sea of parking lots, it resisted floodlighting until

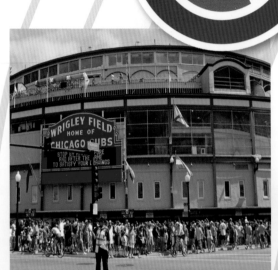

Above and below: Cubs' fans know to check the wind direction as they approach Wrigley Field. It can create a pitchers' park, turning home runs into outs, or into a hitters' heaven, stretching fly balls into homers.

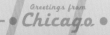

Above: Joe Jackson was the White Sox' best batter when he was banned from the game, accused with seven others of throwing a World Series game in 1919.

1988—forty years after night games were standard elsewhere. The scoreboard is still manually operated. Well-struck balls still lodge in the ivy covering of outfield walls.

It's an image of the game that stirs warm nostalgia in fans, so much so that ballpark designers have now devised a style known as "retro-classic"—green seats, brick and stone in evidence, green-painted girders, asymmetrical lines—reminders of the days of "jewel box" ballparks.

Above: The White Sox' new ballpark opened in 1991 under the name of its predecessor across the street, Comiskey Park.

Left: A home run for Scott Podsednick. He was a noted base stealer for the White Sox.

Right: Southpaw—a reference to the White Sox' location—is the club mascot. He was aboard an Illinois float at President Barack Obama's inauguration.

Football

Pride and power at Soldier Field

Chicago pride has been well served by the Bears. They've played in every season of league football—that's since 1920—and have won more games than any other franchise: almost three-fourths of well over 1,000 games played. The Bears have been NFL champions eight times, Super Bowl winners once; they have the most members in the Pro Football Hall of Fame.

They first appeared as the Decatur Staleys, named for their home town and the starch manufacturer who sponsored them. The founding inspiration was the coach George "Papa Bear" Halas, who became a part-owner and took them to the Chicago Cubs' baseball stadium. Football players are bigger than baseball players, he said, so his team would now be called the Bears.

Halas played as well as coached, to such effect that on a national tour in 1925, the "Monsters of the Midway" attracted crowds of over 70,000 in New York and Los Angeles. Halas was the sole owner of the team by the time it moved to Soldier Field in 1971.

Below and bottom left: Club colors are burnt orange, with navy and white. The helmet "C" has the outline of a wishbone.

Above: "Iron Mike" Ditka was a Bears hero, giving more than twenty years of service as player, assistant coach, and coach. Throughout his career, he won Super Bowls in all three roles.

Right: Soldier Field was built in the 1920s as a city-sponsored sports center. The 67,000-seat inner stadium was built inside the original structure in 2003.

Below: A Green Bay Packer makes the catch. The Bear is free safety Danieal Manning.

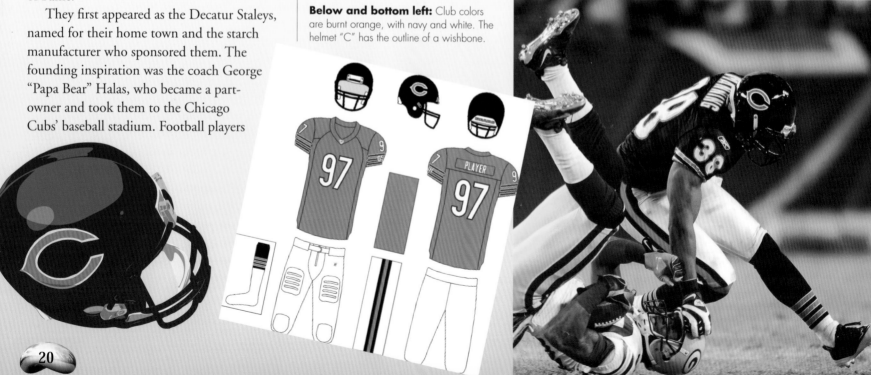

21

Other Sports

Touching all the bases—on ice, turf, and maple

As befits the town regularly nominated as "best sports city" in the United States, Chicago has teams in all five professional major leagues. After the Cubs and White Sox and Bears, there are the Blackhawks for hockey, the basketballing Bulls, and the Chicago Fire soccer team.

Ice hockey was essentially a Canadian game; thus the first American teams were in the border states. Hockey came to Chicago in 1926 when Major Frederick McLaughlin bought one of those squads—from Oregon. He named them the Blackhawks in honor of his World War I military unit. The Blackhawks were the first club to put a team of all American-born players on the ice, and are presently high in the city's estimation as the 2010 winners of the Stanley Cup, the game's top trophy.

Chicago has another hockey team, the Wolves, who play in the American Hockey League. They came to popular attention while they were the one local team to be seen on TV;

Right: Coach John Anderson and his Chicago Wolves celebrate winning the Calder Cup in June 2008. They beat the Scranton Penguins 5–2.

Below: At one time Chicago had six racetracks. This is Arlington Park, home of the Arlington Million, the world's first million-dollar race.

Greetings from
• Chicago •

that was when the Blackhawks' owner tried banning the televising of Hawks' home games in the hope of increasing ticket sales. But the Wolves have not disappointed that audience, being league champions four times.

No such attention-seeking needed by the Chicago Bulls in their heyday. Basketball's most exciting performers won six NBA championships in a span of eight years, led by arguably the most charismatic superstar in all of sport—Michael Jordan.

And appealing to the city's diverse ethnic mix, the outside world's favorite sport, soccer, is played to a high standard in the suburb of Bridgeview. Eastern Europeans and South Americans crowd the roster and the audience for the Chicago Fire who won the sport's two major trophies in their first season, 1998.

Below and below right: The Hawks' Marty Turco (below left) is "the smartest goalie in the NHL." Number 28 (below right) is Center Jake Dowell, playing against the Detroit Red Wings.

Right: Michael Jordan retired. The Bulls slumped. Jordan returned. The Bulls resumed the glory days.

Organized Crime

How a social experiment brought carnage to the streets

Right: Mugshots taken after Al Capone's arrest on a minor contempt charge.

The first street gangs recruited along ethnic lines—Polish, Italian, Irish immigrants taking care of themselves and their ghettoes, terrorizing German, Jewish, and Black newcomers. In return for ballot-stuffing and voter intimidation, ward politicians turned a blind eye to the gangs' growing criminality in docks and stockyard rackets, and in gambling and prostitution.

A vastly lucrative new trade, bootlegging,

Above: The public were ghoulishly fascinated by the details of Al Capone's life, for example, the normality of a fishing trip.

Right: The VIP furnishings of Capone's crumbling prison cell.

Left: His bodyguard, Rocco Fanelli, was seen at the St. Valentine's Day Massacre.

arrived with Prohibition, in 1919. Soon, there was hardly a patch of the city that was not under the "protection" of a gang monopolizing the local booze trade—the Druggan Lake Gang, the Genna Brothers' Gang, Spike O'Donnell, Bugs Moran. The top dogs, though, were John Torrio and his lieutenant,

Above: The gangs brewed beer, imported decent liquor, and distributed the products of backstreet distilleries.

was ever tried for the seven killings that day; Capone, the prime suspect, had the personal alibi of being in Miami at the time.

With the repeal of Prohibition, the gangs concentrated on gambling. Mobsters pervaded the slot machine business and the racing wire services. At the end of the century, drug trafficking was the money spinner, and cyberspace the medium of communication.

Al Capone, and they were not into the notion of profit-sharing.

Violence began in 1923 with the "beer wars." The wars were about whose illicit breweries would supply which illegal speakeasies. The tone for what was to come was set by an early rival to the Torrio/ Capone organization, Frank McErlane, who introduced the Thompson sub-machine gun into criminal armories and used it to become "the most brutal gunman who ever pulled a trigger in Chicago."

Torrio fled town after an assassination attempt; Capone, the new, unchallenged boss, now directed the conflict that resulted in hundreds of killings—cops, attorneys, and newspaper reporters, as well as gangsters—and reached its spectacular climax at the St. Valentine's Day Massacre of 1929. Nobody

Right: Sometimes U.S. agents made a well-publicized "bust." The villainy was not gender-specific; gangsters' women were not merely molls. Here, police raid a female-run gambling den.

Windy City and Politics

Setting the price for a vote

Many of the more cynical clichés about politics emanate from Chicago. "Vote early and often" is a good example, and one which truthfully represented the local scene. Another is "all politics is local politics," and Chicagoans always participated at the grassroots level more intensely than other municipal voters. They were quick to understand how the well-oiled "cogs" of local wards meshed in the great engines of machine politics. They ruefully, amusedly, accepted pervasive corruption; it's the price they paid for "a city that works."

An early preoccupation that sparked riots, fueled electioneering, and rumbled on for twenty years, was liquor laws. Protestant temperance groups ("Yankee elitists") promoted expensive licensing and dry Sundays. Protesting European immigrants discovered that they did indeed have political clout. Liquor laws quietly slunk away.

Those voters were the city's working class, and labor issues were next on their agenda, particularly the brutal strike-breaking practices of the police. The Democrat Carter Harrison made the right promises. Union leaders and radicals mobilized their

Right: Jane Byrne, Chicago's first woman mayor, failed to be the post-Daley reformer many had hoped for.

Below: The moment the anarchist's bomb is thrown in the Haymarket Riot of May 1886, and (inset) speculation about the rioters' arsenal.

Left: New York's Father Knickerbocker wonders whether Chicago can cope with the "white elephant" of the 1893 a Fair.

CHICAGO'S WHITE ELEPHANT.

Above: Newly registered African American voters made Harold Washington mayor. He died in office, in 1987.

Below: Protestors questioned the process of "choosing" a successor.

followers to ensure his election as mayor.

By now, the 1890s, the problem of corruption which would cloud the Chicago scene for the best part of a century was an open sore: wads of cash slipped into judges' pockets; contracts for public services on sale; property tax assessments that favored campaign contributors. This problem would not go away—and, some say, still has not.

Under Mayor Richard J. Daley (1955–76), racial politics anachronistically resurfaced, as he struggled to appease the white middle-class voters who sustained the city's tax base. The aftermath was confusion. There were five different mayors in the next thirteen years. Then Chicago elected Daley's son, Richard M. Daley.

Above and below: Mayor Richard M. Daley, mayor since 1989. His father is seen below with John F. Kennedy; the Chicago Democratic machine was crucial in this presidential campaign.

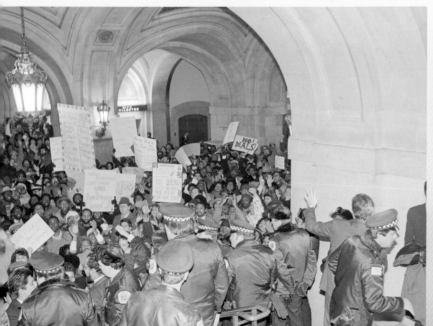

Only in Chicago

Oddities and oddballs in a city of amiable surprises

Chicago has an annual fair that's regularly attended by as many as 2,000 nuns who seem to relish being photographed riding bumper cars and nibbling on cotton candy. There's a favorite chain of grocery stores named Moo & Oink, well-known for a cult late-night TV commercial. The longest-running musical in the city's theatrical history features a song entitled "The Dog Is Eating My Hamster." It's at the Annoyance Theater—only in Chicago.

For gourmets in a hurry to sample the best of everything, there's a dinnertime bus tour— three stops, three courses. Chicago's most notable contribution to world cuisine, the deep dish pizza, has a crust that may be three inches high at the edge; it was devised by Ike Sewell, a former University of Texas football player who yearned for extra filling. For the Saturday before Thanksgiving, they hang a million lights on 200 trees along North Michigan Avenue, beside the lake. That's the signal for longer store-opening hours befitting the holiday season.

It's a city that delights in idiosyncracy and eccentricity, and having a good time. The Free Fair that the nuns attend gives everyone the chance to be a winner—as fast-crawling babies, at egg-rolling, chicken-eating, growing the longest pigtails, and owning the cutest pet. At the Lincoln Park Zoo, volunteers create a Halloween event particularly for poorer children. Up to 30,000 attend the Spooky Zoo Spectacular.

Right: Stunt pilots, formation flyers, parachutists, and water and jet skiers perform for the annual Chicago Air and Water Show. With the lake shore offering perfect viewing, up to 3,000,000 spectators enjoy the displays.

Below: Tourboat passengers on the Chicago River will be told how it used to flow in the other direction—and how it's dyed green every year for St. Patrick's Day.

ST. PATRICK'S DAY PARADE

Navy Pier

The year-round playground that highlights the water

The lake was so important to Chicago that the visionary architect Daniel Burnham's *Plan of Chicago* proposed the building of five piers. That was in 1909. By the time the first, and only, pier was built and the gloomy restrictions of World War I had been lifted, the lake's commercial traffic was in decline: trucks were taking the freight business on to the highways, and steamboat passengers were becoming car owners.

The way was clear for the creation of what has become the Midwest's favorite pleasure ground. This man-made promontory morphed into a park of fairground rides and picnics cooled by lake breezes, where the shipping is pleasure boats and cruisers, and working Chicago is observed from the capsules of a slow-turning Ferris wheel. Daniel Burnham would have approved that his Municipal Pier #2 became the People's Pier.

Above left: The "Captain on the Helm" a sculpture by Michael Martino welcomes visitors to the historic Navy Pier.

Above right: Navy Pier, built in 1916, is Chicago's number one tourist attraction.

Below: The pier and its grounds now occupy more than 50 acres.

Millennium Park

Mayor Daley commissions the world's largest rooftop garden

Above: The Crown Fountain by Jaume Plensa. Light-emitting diodes behind two 50-foot-high walls of glass bricks show digital videos.

Below left: Millennium Park's Pritzker Pavilion (foreground), named for Chicago business leader Jay Pritzker.

Below right: Cloud Gate, the 33-foot-high "bean" of stainless steel, distorts as it reflects, producing popular photo opportunities. No seams show between the 168 plates.

For the city's millennium marker, Mayor Richard M. Daley proposed to use the air rights over a former railyard complex as the basis of a 24-acre park. It would be a public-private-sectors project. Basic costs would be about $150 million; private and corporate benefactors would pay for "enhancements." In the end, approaching $500 million was spent—and the city had set an example for modern, humane urban planning.

The extraordinary donor response included more than eighty private gifts of $1 million or more, and with that sort of money in the account, ambitions soared. Frank Gehry, by now the most celebrated architect in the world, was hired. He was promised $15 million to pay for a bandshell. The park's features took the names of their sponsors. Gehry's assignment was the Pritzker Pavilion. The AT&T Plaza hosts the Cloud Gate sculpture by Anish Kapoor, which cost four times more than the original estimate of $6 million. A Chicago family put their name to the Crown Fountain. Ann Lurie, wealthy from real estate, gave a $10 million endowment for the care of Lurie Garden.

And so on: McCormick Tribune Plaza, BP Bridge, Harris Theater, and Wrigley Square.

It was like the olden, golden days of Chicago philanthropy a century before.

Wish You Were Here

A second city with first-class credentials

In the middle of the country, and the hub of the nation's transport systems, Chicago flaunts power and wealth with dazzling skyscrapers and immaculate mansions, and is a kaleidoscope of races and cultures. No wonder Chicago became a compelling destination. Twelve million visitors to the World's Colombian Exposition of 1893 thought so, and the traffic has continued ever since. Conventioneers and business people, small-town Midwesterners and international admirers—they all have plenty to write about on the postcards home.

Above: The greeting card lettering is big and bold, as are the visions of Chicago. One estimate indicates 40 million visitors each year come to admire them.

The Wrigley building on North Michigan Avenue
© Alamy

POST CARD

PLACE
STAMP
HERE

_____

_____

_____

_____

Chicago's State Street at night, 1953
© Corbis

POST CARD

PLACE
STAMP
HERE

_____

_____

_____

_____

Flags fly in Chicago's State Street in 1926
© Alamy

POST CARD

PLACE
STAMP
HERE

_____

_____

_____

_____

Chicago cityscape at dusk
© Corbis

POST CARD

PLACE
STAMP
HERE

_____

_____

_____

_____